W0036636

AN ANTHOLOGY OF

Christmas

Written by Auriol Bishop

Illustrated by Angela Rizza
and Daniel Long

Introduction

If we could join Father Christmas in his sleigh for a trip around the world, we'd learn that our favourite things about Christmas probably depend on where we live. Perhaps you are close to the North Pole, like the reindeer, and December is a month of snow and ice and long, dark nights. Or perhaps you are more like the penguin and live nearer the South Pole, where Christmas comes on a bright, sunny, endless summer's day.

This book is a Christmas adventure through nature, full of fascinating facts and magical myths to help you celebrate this most wonderful time of the year. Did you know that as well as the Christmas tree, the brightest, most beautiful star, and a donkey, there is also a Christmas cat, a spider's web, and even a cactus? I wonder what other surprises you will find!

Auriol B.

Auriol Bishop
Author

Contents

Holly

Long before Father Christmas, the mythical Holly King ruled winter. With its spiny leaves that act as miniature lightning conductors, this ancient guardian of the woodlands holds a very special kind of magic. And some believe that if you bring the leaves inside in winter, they provide shelter for the fairies.

Even in the coldest, darkest days of the year, when many other trees are bare of leaves and fruit, the holly tree shines with its glossy green leaves and bright red berries, giving food to birds and shelter for animals and colour to the hedgerows. Caterpillars chomp on the leaves, building their strength to transform into holly blue butterflies, and bees love the four-petalled little white flowers in spring.

Deer nibble at the holly's topmost, youngest leaves before their protective prickles grow.

Ivy

Fast-growing ivy grows on trees, without harming them, and provides support for many different species of wildlife.

Blackbirds rely on ivy's rich black berries to see them through the hungry months.

It is said that wreathing your house in ivy garlands will keep the goblins away!

Ivy creeps along the ground until it finds a tree to climb. Then it uses little hairs to cling on tight, and up it goes until it reaches the light. There, it transforms. Its distinctive five-pointed leaves become heart-shaped and it bursts into bloom — with spherical, bobbly flowers that look like little green firework explosions.

Nectar oozes from the ivy flowers to provide one final feast to buzzing crowds of bees and wasps, flies and hoverflies before they tuck up to sleep for the winter; brimstone and comma butterflies store up their energy ready to hibernate, protected by ivy's leathery leaves. No matter how severe the weather, ivy is never damaged by frost, and starlings and sparrows, bats and robins all find a cosy haven behind its evergreen curtain.

Robin redbreast

With their bright red chests and little round heads, robin redbreasts are such jolly birds it's no surprise they are the bird of Christmas. Oddly enough, while these European robins are friendly garden birds in Britain and Ireland, they are shyer creatures in other parts of the continent, where they prefer to stay safely tucked away in hedgerows.

A robin's idea of a delicious feast is a plump, fresh worm or crispy insect, and they love to perch nearby when you are digging in the garden to see what treats might be revealed. They sing a special song in wintertime, to let other robins know where to find them — and their trills can sound as pretty as a Christmas carol. An old story tells that in the cold of the stable where Jesus was born, a little brown robin fanned the dying fire, coming so close to the flames that it burned its breast bright red, and in her gratitude Mary named it the most sacred of birds.

Thanks to Christmas cards, European robins can be spotted all over the world!

The European robin's eggs are creamy coloured with light-brown speckles.

Almonds

Early-blossoming almonds are a symbol of hope, prized for their sweet nuts and nourishing oil, while sugared almonds are a popular Christmas tradition.

Dates

The Qur'an tells that Jesus was born under the shade of a date palm tree. More than a thousand dates can grow in a single cluster, tucked under the crown of leaves that tops the tall trunk of the date palm.

Chestnuts

Soft, nutritious chestnuts can be ground into flour to make bread or pasta, pickled in syrup, or candied as sweets, and are most delicious roasted on an open fire!

Chestnuts are held within a protective spikey jacket.

Pomegranate

This fruit is prized as the jewel of foods in many ancient myths. Rejoice on Yalda Night, an Iranian festival celebrating the winter solstice, by cracking open the hard, round outer husk and feasting on the treasure chest of juicy seeds within.

Grapes

Eaten fresh from the bunch, dried into raisins, or fermented to make wine, grapes are some of the oldest and the most popular fruit in the world.

Starfruit

The leaves of the starfruit tree are very sensitive: they fold up if they're touched, or in strong winds. Its rich, amber-coloured fruits make beautiful, bittersweet stars when cut into slices.

Fruits and nuts

Stir-Up Sunday is a traditional day in the UK for making Christmas pudding, mixing fruits together from all over the world.

We have been feasting on fruits and nuts since human life began. Fruits are the part of a plant that holds the seeds. And nuts are fruits with a hard outer shell, with an edible kernel inside. Plants grow tasty, fleshy fruits to tempt us — and other animals — to eat them and help the plant spread its seeds.

In the cold winters of the northern hemisphere, where many Christmas traditions began, fresh food was scarce, so recipes for the festive feast called for fruits and nuts that had been picked and preserved in times of plenty, or could be transported from distant, sunnier climes.

Walnuts

Walnuts are hard to open! An old German story tells that a puppet-maker won a prize by inventing the first nutcracker doll with strong, wide jaws perfect for cracking the tough shells and getting to the tasty nut inside.

Hazelnuts

Dormice eat hazelnuts to fatten up for hibernation, and squirrels love them too. All kinds of birds flock to feast on the little round nuts of this magical tree, which in Ireland was known as the Tree of Knowledge.

Snow

Snowflakes have no colour, but the way the light passes through them makes the snow appear white to our eyes.

Snow falls like little tiny stars from the sky, formed when microscopic ice crystals cluster around specks of dust or pollen in the clouds, until they get so heavy that they tumble down to earth. Snowflakes are symmetrical, and hexagonal — ornate branches of ice radiate from the centre, each with smaller branches of their own, in repeating patterns called fractals.

It hardly ever snows in the mild, Mediterranean climate of Bethlehem, where Jesus was born. But the colder regions of the northern hemisphere are covered with snow for many months of the year, and it is said that Father Christmas lives in the snowy North Pole, where Christmas falls in the heart of winter. So perhaps that is why his magical sleigh scatters a trail of snow wherever he goes!

A snowflake's shape depends on how fast it falls, where it lands, and if there is a wind blowing — which means that each one is unique.

Wild boar

Ancient king of the woodlands, the wild boar has muscles as tough as armour and long, sharp, curved tusks. They help the boar to plough the ground and tear through thickets — and fight off their enemies! Boars' coats are designed for camouflage, blending with the shade so they can sleep undisturbed all day, hidden in bracken and bramble beneath the trees. They wake at dusk, to have a good old wallow and wash in wet mud before their night's hunting.

Gullinbursti, the golden-bristled boar of Norse myth, is the bringer of a bountiful harvest. And in medieval times, a fearsome boar's head was the centrepiece of the grandest feasts, a shiny red apple in its mouth and sometimes, for Christmas, adorned with a golden crown.

Baby boarlets are known as "humbugs", because they are striped like the minty sweets!

Wild boar snuffle out tasty worms, grubs, fungus, and roots to eat, digging deep in the dirt with their strong round snouts.

Star of Bethlehem

In the year Jesus was born, Chinese astronomers recorded something special in their observations of the sky. A beautiful, bright star caught their eye — so bright that they described it as a "tail-less comet", although unlike other comets, this star did not move.

There are many theories about the "Star in the East" that, the Bible tells us, was followed by the Wise Men to Bethlehem. Perhaps it was a sighting of the star Regulus when it aligned with the planets Jupiter and Venus. Perhaps it was so very bright because it was a nova — two stars coming together in a tremendous explosion that gets a million times brighter for a while before fading away again.

It is thought that the Wise
Men may have been astrologers.

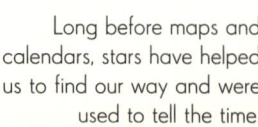

Long before maps and
calendars, stars have helped
us to find our way and were
used to tell the time.

Poinsettia is known as *flor de nochebuena* – the Christmas Eve flower.

Poinsettia

Poinsettias like to be warm and cosy. In their sunny homelands of Mexico — where their true name of cuetlaxóchitl means "flower that perishes like all that is pure" — these flame-leaved plants can grow as tall as a tree.

Their flowers are a tight cluster of little yellow buds surrounded by large, wide, bright red leaves which have the special name of bracts. The bracts only turn red for a few weeks in winter, when there is plenty of light during the day, and the nights are long and dark. Butterflies and hummingbirds love to feed on poinsettia pollen. Believing these beautiful creatures to be the spirits of great warriors, the Aztecs of Mesoamerica would leave the flowers as offerings to them.

The colour and vibrancy of the poinsettia is determined by the amount of light it gets.

Reindeer

With feet like snow shoes, reindeer are among the fastest runners on earth, and a baby reindeer can run almost as soon as it is born! Both male and female reindeer grow great antlers on their heads, for protection.

Reindeer live in the freezing polar and mountain regions of the Arctic tundra, and boreal forests of Europe and North America. To help them survive, they have a double coat of fur that is woolly underneath with long, tubular hairs above. These hollow hairs give them buoyancy, helping them swim through icy rivers. The fur changes colour with the seasons, for camouflage. A reindeer's eyes change colour too: from golden in the summer, to blue in the winter, adjusting to the different types of light.

A reindeer's antlers are made of bone, and when they are new they are covered in soft velvet.

Reindeer calves can walk, run, and travel with their mothers within a few hours of being born.

Wheat

Grains have been farmed for food all over the world since Neolithic times. And in Scandinavia it is a tradition to give thanks for the harvest by saving the first, the last — or the best! — bundle of dried grain-grasses to make a Christmas treat for the animals.

Wheat, oats, corn, rice, and bamboo are all types of grass. They like plenty of light and rain, and the seeds can lie dormant to save their energy when it's too cold to grow. Woken by the warmth of sunlight, they send up tall green shoots topped by spikelets of seeds. A handful of wheat seeds, saved from the harvest and planted in a shallow dish to nurture indoors so that they sprout into grass just in time for Christmas, is said to bring blessings for the year to come.

Tie a bundle of wheat with red ribbon and hang it outside — if lots of little birds visit they'll bring you luck!

For humans to eat wheat, it has to be hulled to take off the hard outside husks. But birds love to peck on the seeds just as they are!

Sheep

Sheep love family, and hate to be away from their flock. Thousands of years ago, they were tamed and bred in the lands of western Asia and North Africa known as the Fertile Crescent, and have brought us gifts of wool, milk, and meat ever since.

Sheep need to be free to roam and graze for food, which they nibble by plucking leaves and flowers with their specially split lip. They eat fast, and digest slowly, resting and ruminating to chew on the cud. The shepherds who tend them use a special call or even a song to guide their flock of sheep to new pastures. On the night of the Nativity, the Bible says that shepherds watching their flocks in the sandy hills near Bethlehem heard the news of Jesus's birth from a glorious vision of angels.

Nomadic Bedouin shepherds still live and travel with their herds of sheep today.

Studded with fragrant cloves, oranges make scented pomander decorations.

Oranges

As round as the sun and gleaming like gold, oranges are little gifts of light. From their birthplace in the Himalayan foothills in Asia, these precious fruits have travelled the world — saving the lives of sailors at sea, giving a colour its name, and brightening up even the darkest of times.

Bees love the delicate white blossoms of the orange tree — but apparently elephants really don't like oranges at all! Peeling an orange is like unwrapping a present to find lots of smaller presents inside: its juicy inner pulp is divided into segments to break up and share.

Oranges glowing in the sunshine of the Algarve, Portugal.

27

The wintry boreal forest regions of the world are named after Boreas, the Greek god of the cold north wind.

Norway spruce

Towering tall in northern snow forests, the Norway spruce is decorated by nature all year round, with long cones that stand tall as candles or dangle like diamond-patterned baubles.

Goldcrests and long-tailed tits perch on its swaying branches, and red squirrels scamper round its trunk. Known as the "tree of the night" and the "tree of shadows", it is a favourite roost of the boreal owl, and is devoted to Artemis, Greek goddess of the hunt and the moon. Lapland legends tell that Kuusi the spruce tree is sacred to Tapio the forest god, and hunters would sleep under its roof-like branches for shelter at night. It is said that the serene spruce forest gives the best echoes, and its resonant wood is the secret to making a perfect violin.

Snow-white snowshoe hares reach up to nibble at the sweet young tips of the needles of the Norway spruce.

The Norway spruce is a much-loved traditional Christmas tree – the evergreen emblem of protection and the return of new life.

Yew tree
Ancient symbol of hope and celebration, yew tree boughs were once made into little indoor trees and garlands decorated with treats and toys.

Christmas trees

There's a story that starlight twinkling on frost-covered fir trees inspired the first Christmas tree candlelights. Right below the Arctic Circle, the northernmost forests of the world are filled with conifers that grow in symmetrical pyramid shapes with pointy tips to help them stand tall, even under the weight of the heaviest snow.

Christmas in the northern hemisphere is celebrated on the coldest days of winter. But in the tropical and desert regions of the southern hemisphere, it falls on the long hot days of midsummer, when plants are a blooming riot of festive colours. So Christmas trees can look very different, depending on where you are in the world.

Inkberry tree
People of the Virgin Islands have used this prickly evergreen as a Christmas tree. The name "inkberry" comes from the dark purple juice contained in its white berries, once used to make ink.

Douglas fir
A popular Christmas tree native to North America, the Douglas fir has long, distinctive-shaped cones, and a thick, red-brown armour of bark that protects it from frost and fire.

Cotton plant

Native to South and Central America, the cotton plant has been cultivated for thousands of years. Fluffy cotton fibres burst out of the dried seed pods, called bolls — and look just like soft snowballs that will never melt! Cotton is a popular Christmas decoration in Argentina.

To the Noongar Aboriginal peoples of Western Australia, the moodjar is a spirit tree, and its sacred flowers must never be picked.

Pohutukawa

The awe-inspiring pohutukawa tree shares its Maori name with a star. Bursting into bright crimson flowers for December, this Christmas tree lives by the ocean. It climbs cliffs, and sprouts roots from its trunk.

Moodjar

Known as Western Australia's Christmas tree because of its spectacular golden blooms at Christmas time, the mighty moodjar isn't actually a tree at all — it's mistletoe!

Donkeys have a distinctive cross-mark in the fur on their backs, which some say is a holy blessing.

Donkey

Donkeys hate to be alone. They are wonderful wayfinders and guardians, with long ears that help them hear danger, and a unique braying HEE-HAW that can be heard for many miles around. Donkeys are strong and determined, and calm in the face of danger. It is said they can tell how you're feeling from the sound of your heart.

Since ancient times, and still today, donkeys have been ridden by shepherds and carried packs for travellers, making paths where no other forms of transport can reach. In Christmas tales, donkeys help to carry presents. Santa Lucia (Saint Lucy) visits Italy riding her faithful flying donkey Gastaldo. In France, the donkey companion of Père Noël (Father Christmas) is named Gui — which means "mistletoe" in French. Line up your shoes by the fireplace and fill them with carrots or apples for the donkeys, and they might leave you some treats in return!

Mary may have ridden a donkey
on the long journey from her home in
Nazareth to Bethlehem, where Jesus was born.

Mistletoe

Celtic druids are said to have harvested mistletoe branches with a golden sickle to create a charm.

These brambling birds are enjoying feeding from the berries of the mistletoe.

Mistletoe loves to live in apple trees. And birds love to feast on mistletoe! In Anglo-Saxon, "mistletoe" means "dung-on-a-twig", as the birds eating the berries leave behind plenty of droppings! Inside the plump, pearl-white berries there is a special glue-like substance, and when the bird poops it out, the seeds stick on the branch below, where they grow into a small, woody shrub, magically suspended between the earth and the sky.

Balder, the Norse god of light, died when he was struck by a dart made out of mistletoe. Heartbroken, Frigg, the goddess of love and beauty, persuaded the other gods to bring him back to life — and repaid their kindness with kisses. Perhaps this is why, today, we stand under the mistletoe in hope of a kiss!

The ancient Romans hung mistletoe over doorways to protect their buildings.

Partridge

The partridge is a bird that prefers to run... If a fox comes slinking by, they will run quickly for shelter — only whirring into a burst of flight if the danger gets too close. Plump and rotund, partridges like to stay on the ground, living together in family groups called coveys. They even build their nests by scraping a dip amongst the meadow grasses, and their chicks can run from the moment they hatch.

Ancient Greek myths tell of a young man saved from death by falling when the goddess Athena transformed him into a partridge, which forevermore huddles safe in the hedges and avoids high places. According to the famous song, on the first day of Christmas, "my true love" gave a partridge in a pear tree as a gift. The loyal partridge mates for life, and pear trees can live for up to 250 years, making this the perfect present to promise true love!

The partridge can move surprisingly quickly on its short stubby legs.

Partridges prefer to
stay on the ground,
and – despite the song –
are not known to live
in pear trees!

Oak

Oak trees play an important part in Slavic Christmas celebrations.

In the wild, wood-covered lands of long ago, trees were sacred beings — and none more so than the mighty oak. Oaks can live for many hundreds of years, and their great trunks and wide-spreading branches are home to whole ecosystems of small creatures. Even their roots and the rich earth beneath create the perfect place for beetles to burrow and squirrels to forage. Bats roost in the nooks of its rough, craggy bark, and colourful jays love to steal its cupped acorns, which fall to the ground in the autumn to provide a fine feast for badgers and deer, wild boar and wood mice.

The oak is often struck by lightning, and was known as the tree of the thunder gods Dagda, Zeus, Jupiter, and Thor. In Serbia, a specially chosen oak log is burned on the Christmas fire, and it is believed that if lots of sparks fly up, then much happiness, money, and joy will come.

Legends tell of the Oak King ruling the summer months, and at the winter solstice fighting a mighty battle with his brother the Holly King.

In many European cultures, oak trees represent strength and wisdom.

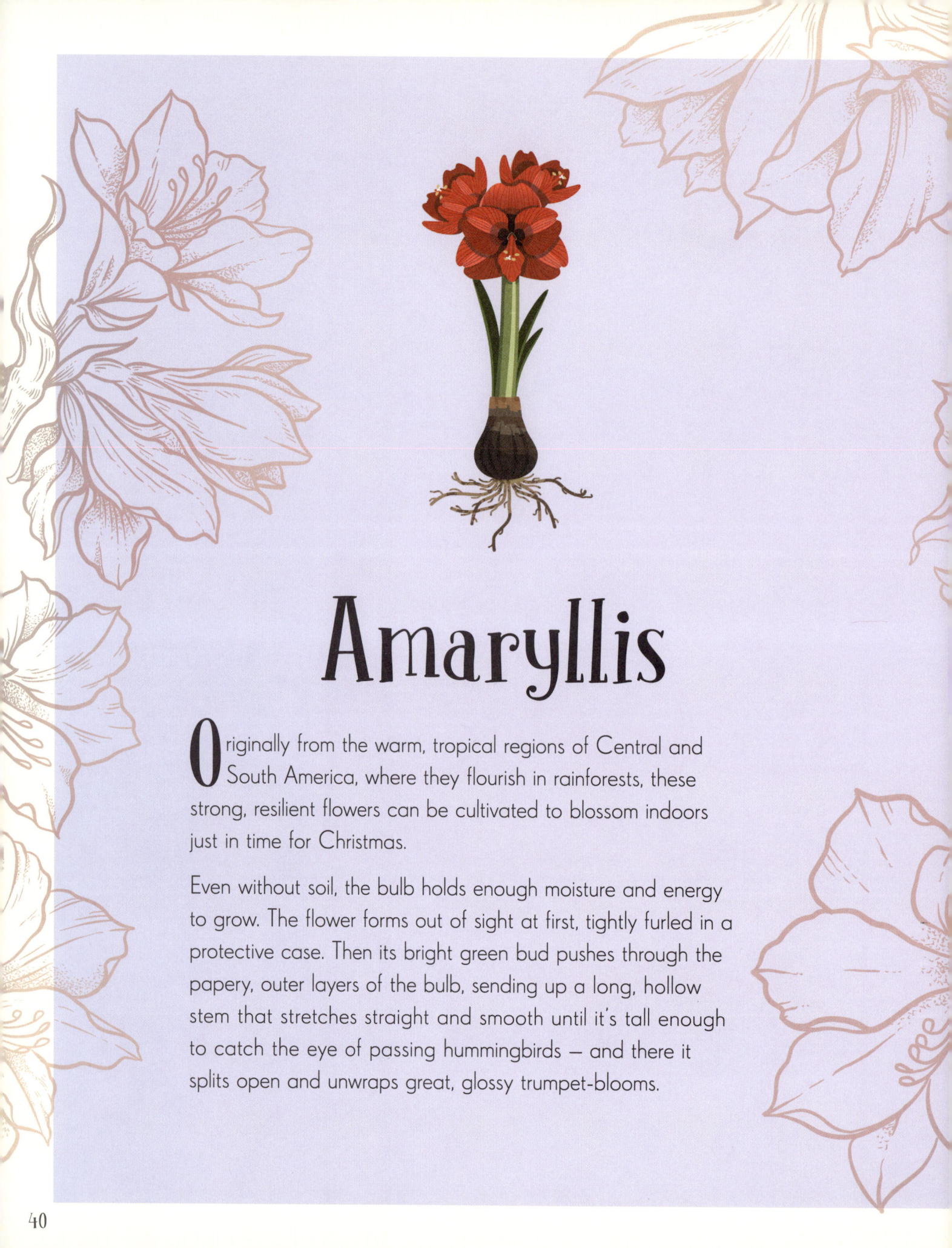

Amaryllis

Originally from the warm, tropical regions of Central and South America, where they flourish in rainforests, these strong, resilient flowers can be cultivated to blossom indoors just in time for Christmas.

Even without soil, the bulb holds enough moisture and energy to grow. The flower forms out of sight at first, tightly furled in a protective case. Then its bright green bud pushes through the papery, outer layers of the bulb, sending up a long, hollow stem that stretches straight and smooth until it's tall enough to catch the eye of passing hummingbirds — and there it splits open and unwraps great, glossy trumpet-blooms.

Here you can see the bright green shoot pushing up and out through the brown amaryllis bulb.

An amaryllis bulb is a present that opens itself, like a slow-motion jack-in-a-box.

Turkey

With its dramatic plumage, the turkey is truly a bird that inspires celebration! Turkeys express themselves with every part of their being. The bright "snood" tassel of loose skin that bobbles above their beaks, as well as the whole of their bald, featherless head and the folding wattles and caruncles that cover their necks, can change shape and colour — from white to red to blue — to show their mood.

Turkeys flap their gleaming, dark bronze wings to dance and fight, and male turkey cocks have magnificent tailfans that they use to show off, puffing their feathers and strutting, dragging their wings like a cape, and making loud gobbling and drumming sounds that can be heard for miles around.

The Aztecs of Mesoamerica worshipped the turkey as a god.

The turkey's bold-patterned, iridescent feathers are waterproof and help them keep warm in winter.

Ginger

This spice grows from a thick, underground stem called a rhizome. Ginger has been used for centuries to add a fiery kick to food and drinks, and it is a common ingredient in traditional medicine in many countries, including China and India.

The Sanskrit name for ginger, *sringavera* means "root shaped like a horn".

Perhaps the first gingerbread houses were inspired by the witch's house in the Grimms' fairy tale *Hansel and Gretel...*

Spices

Spices have stories to tell of adventure and rarity, battles and survival, feasts and celebrations. They travel all over the world, and come from precious plants that have been prized for many thousands of years for their power to heal, to preserve, and for their divine scents and opulent flavours.

Sometimes, spices are ground to a fine powder. Other spices are hard and dry, and cannot be eaten. They are infused in drinks, stirred deep into puddings, or sprinkled with sugar on sweets.

Star anise

It may be shaped like a flower, but star anise is actually a fruit used as a spice. The fruits, stems, leaves, and petals of star anise all contain essential oils, and it is said to have health-giving properties. Star anise can be hung as decorations, and as a protective lucky charm.

Nutmeg

In spite of its name, nutmeg is not a nut at all! It is the kernel of the fruit from the *Myristica fragrans* tree, native only to an archipelago of tiny volcanic islands in a remote stretch of Indonesia's Banda Sea. Nutmeg was once the rarest of spices.

Cloves

Picked by hand from the *cengkeh* tree, cloves are flower buds. The tradition of sticking them into oranges to make a pomander began in medieval times, when cloves were thought to ward off the plague.

Fragrant spices are the delicious smell of Christmas.

Cinnamon

This spice comes from tree bark. It is carefully peeled from the small, evergreen kurudu tree in the lush forests of Sri Lanka. The spice is valued for its sweet perfume, and for its use in cooking and medicine.

When cinnamon dries, it rolls up tight into "quills".

Saffron

The name "saffron" comes from the Arabic word for yellow. It grows from the heart of the purple *Crocus sativus* flower. From ancient times, saffron has been prized as an expensive yellow dye, for its fabled medicinal powers, and for the intense colour, flavour, and aroma that it brings to cooking.

While some say the Yule cat is black as a starless night, others say it is tiger-striped and bearded, like this Norwegian forest cat.

Cat

Cats are fierce hunters, prowling on soft-padded paws and pouncing on their unsuspecting prey. Every bone and sinew of their powerful bodies is built for the hunt, from their night-vision eyes and extra-sensory whiskers, to their pointed fangs and retractable claws, all the way down their sinuous spine, to the end of their ominously twitching tail.

The Norse goddess Freyja rode through the sky in a golden chariot drawn by two white long-haired cats. The Japanese maneki-neko "beckoning-cat" will bring you luck. But Icelandic tales tell of a terrifying feline, bigger than houses, that gobbles up anyone without new clothes to keep them warm in winter. So be glad when you get socks for Christmas: they're keeping you safe from the Yule cat!

In Iceland at Christmas time, a demon Yule cat is said to stalk the streets...

Spider's web

It is lucky to find
a spider on your
Christmas tree!

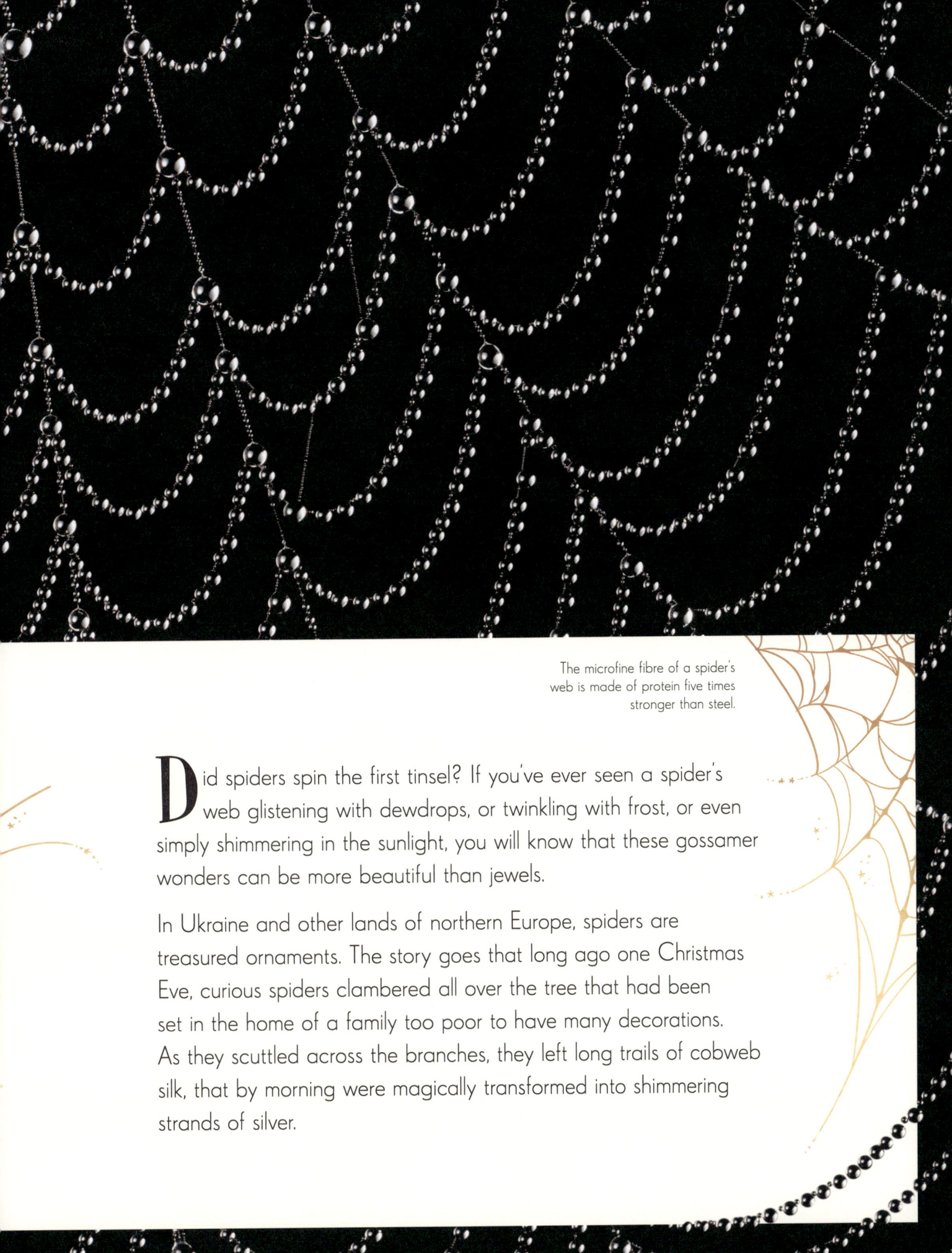

The microfine fibre of a spider's
web is made of protein five times
stronger than steel.

Did spiders spin the first tinsel? If you've ever seen a spider's
web glistening with dewdrops, or twinkling with frost, or even
simply shimmering in the sunlight, you will know that these gossamer
wonders can be more beautiful than jewels.

In Ukraine and other lands of northern Europe, spiders are
treasured ornaments. The story goes that long ago one Christmas
Eve, curious spiders clambered all over the tree that had been
set in the home of a family too poor to have many decorations.
As they scuttled across the branches, they left long trails of cobweb
silk, that by morning were magically transformed into shimmering
strands of silver.

Dried cranberries are often used to make Christmas wreaths and garlands.

Cranberries

Did you know that cranberries grow in bogs where spiders protect them from insects? These bright, bouncing berries come from small, creeping vines that flourish in the acidic marshes and spongy peat left behind when the glaciers of North America melted, around 15,000 years ago.

Within each cranberry, there are four air pockets, and when the bog floods in the autumn rains, the berries float free from the vines, carrying their seeds to find new spots to grow. Their guardians, the wolf spiders, feed on cranberry fruit worms and weevils, lying in wait just beneath the water's surface and pouncing on their unsuspecting prey.

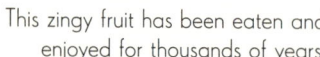

This zingy fruit has been eaten and enjoyed for thousands of years.

Ox

Many nativity scenes show oxen watching over the newborn baby Jesus.

A herd of wild gaur — a relative of domestic oxen — drinking from a watering hole in India.

Strong and calm, oxen are tame cattle, patiently raised and trained to work the land. They move at a slow and steady pace to haul heavy loads and plough fields for planting. Their two-toed hooves help them balance and grip on uneven ground, and they are shod with special half-moon shoes of iron to protect their feet.

When they're not working, oxen are most content to lie in the quiet of an ox barn, peacefully chewing the cud. There was no cradle in the stable where Jesus was born, so the Bible tells that instead Mary laid her new baby in the animals' food-rack, known as a manger, filled with soft, sweet-smelling hay.

Northern cardinals are said
to be messenger birds, heralding visitors or
bringing reminders of good fortune and love.

Northern cardinal

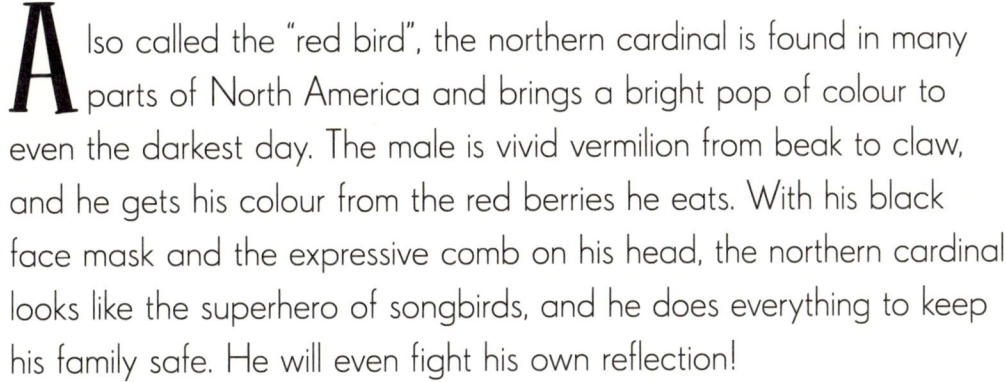

While lacking the bright-red plumage of the male, the female northern cardinal has her own gentle beauty, and her soft, brown feathers are tinged with red.

Also called the "red bird", the northern cardinal is found in many parts of North America and brings a bright pop of colour to even the darkest day. The male is vivid vermilion from beak to claw, and he gets his colour from the red berries he eats. With his black face mask and the expressive comb on his head, the northern cardinal looks like the superhero of songbirds, and he does everything to keep his family safe. He will even fight his own reflection!

Cardinals use singing as their superpower. The female will call for food from the nest, or to let her mate know there's danger nearby. Pairs of cardinals duet together, and defend their territory by belting out their song.

Northern cardinals only flock together in wintertime, a sure sign that something wonderful is about to happen – Christmas is near!

Beware – tradition warns that if you've been unkind, you might find a lump of coal, instead of treats, in your Christmas stocking!

Coal

Coal is the favourite gift of goblins and demons! The energy in coal is the energy of the sun, trapped by dead plants and transformed over hundreds of millions of years into rock – a very light rock that catches fire!

Underground fires are known to burn for many years where coal has spontaneously combusted beneath the surface of the earth. You might think that coal is a disappointing thing to find in your Christmas stocking, but at the time of the Industrial Revolution, this sooty rock was known as "black gold". It powered everything from train engines to factories, and later brought light and heat to homes across the world.

It's not possible to make more coal once the earth's supplies are all used up — so perhaps one day a piece of coal will be a rare and precious gem.

The North Pole is at the heart of the Arctic Circle:
the polar desert regions that cover the top of the
earth with vast white plains of snow dunes and
icebergs, glaciers and frost-covered tundra.

North Pole

There is no land at the North Pole — only the fathomless depths of the Arctic Ocean, constantly covered in frozen sea ice. Polaris, the North Star, shines in the sky above, and from this northernmost part of our planet, all directions are south.

Here, the dark, winter nights are long, and on the winter solstice the sun won't rise above the horizon at all. The cold polar nights are marked with feasting and celebrations to greet the returning sun — and there are many tales told of the spirits who rule in the dead of winter...

For the Sami peoples of the Arctic, the long polar nights are full of danger, when fireside tales warn that the Northern Lights might steal you away.

Penguin chicks each have a distinctive call that helps their parents recognize them.

Penguin

For penguins, Christmas comes in the summertime. These birds live in the southern hemisphere, where the December solstice falls on the longest, sunniest day of the year.

Soft, downy penguin chicks hatch by the light of the midnight sun, "pipping" their way through the eggshell with a special "egg tooth". Penguins are found on every continent south of the equator — from the rocky shores of the tropical Galápagos Islands to the emperor penguins and Adélies who live in the extreme cold of Antarctica — the largest single piece of ice on earth. Penguins don't fly — but they are the best swimmers and deepest divers of all birds. Flapping their strong wings like flippers, they "fly" through the water, leaping above the waves to breathe. And they can toboggan too, sliding across the ice on their tummies!

A penguin's Christmas dinner is fishy krill — regurgitated specially by their parents!

White doves are a
symbol of peace
and goodwill.

A beautiful white fantail dove
flies through the air.

Dove

In the wild, doves often live in sea caves and cliff faces. They come in all kinds of colours — from silver-grey to dark black, orange-brown to pinky-white, or sometimes a combination, with bands of iridescent purple and green. They belong to a large family of birds called columbidae that also includes the now-extinct dodo and the very-much-alive flocks of pigeons found in towns and cities across the world.

Pairs of doves will coo and trill to one another, and cuddle together. It is said that Ashtarte, the Syrian goddess of love, was hatched from an egg tended by doves. On the second day of Christmas, "my true love" gifted two turtle doves. Perhaps, next time you see a pigeon, you will think of it as a messenger of love!

Legend has it that the Wise Men rode on camels to visit baby Jesus, though the Bible does not actually mention this.

Camel

If you live in the desert, there's no better friend to have than a camel. From their air-cooling noses to their splayed, padded toes, camels are built to survive in some of the most extreme conditions on the planet.

Creamy-pale, golden, or almost-black, a camel's thick fur coat acts like a blanket — keeping it warm in the freezing-cold desert nights and cool in the blistering heat of the day. Two rows of extra-long eyelashes and three eyelids protect their eyes from blinding sandstorms, and their leathery lips and tongues mean they can eat the prickly desert plants without hurting their mouths.

Camels are treasured as a gift from Allah in Arab cultures, and many miraculous tales are told of their adventures.

The one-humped dromedary, or Arabian, camel has been domesticated for over 3,000 years.

The Wise Men would have presented their gifts in beautifully crafted containers almost as precious as what was inside.

Three gifts

Gold

This soft, shiny metal comes from outer space. Gold is formed by cosmic explosions when stars collapse, and was delivered to earth on meteorites. It is mined from "veins" in the earth's crust and mantle. In some places, it has been found by sifting water on riverbeds and sandy shores.

Myrrh

This pale yellow resin seeps from wounds in the bark of the thorny *Commiphora* tree and turns reddish-brown as it hardens. Myrrh has been used for centuries as a perfume, anointing oil, and medicine — being crushed into ointments to soothe burns and wounds. The ancient Egyptians used myrrh to embalm mummies.

The Christmas story tells us that Wise Men — the Magi — came journeying from the East, following the brightest star to visit a newborn baby king. They brought with them precious gifts: regal gold, sacred frankincense, and healing myrrh. I wonder, what gift would you have brought?

Gold is renowned for its great value all over the world. But what about frankincense and myrrh? They're probably not on anyone's wish list to Father Christmas! Long ago though, when Jesus was born, they were rare and expensive treasures. And Mary would have been glad of these thoughtful gifts. In traditional Asian medicine, frankincense and myrrh are given to mothers to help them heal after their baby is born.

Frankincense

A resin, frankincense comes from the thick, milky-white juice that oozes from the leafy *Boswellia sacra* tree to protect itself when cuts are made in its trunk. The resin hardens into aromatic "teardrops" used by people across the world in medicine, cosmetics, perfumes, and sacred rituals.

Goat

Is the Christmas goat naughty — or nice? Certainly, goats look rather like mythical beasts! Their wide, staring eyes have oblong, horizontal pupils that let them see all around. Their cloven hooves have grippy pads and sharp dewclaws that cling to sheer cliffs which seem impossible to climb. They rear up on their back legs to reach for food — or to fight. And when they headbutt with their curving horns, it may be they want to play, or it could be a warning...

In Nordic lands at Christmas time, Yule spirits take the form of goats. The fearsome man-goat Krampus rampages through the towns, and Julebukk the trickster Yule goat may come knocking at your door, demanding treats. Or if you've been good, you might get a visit from the jovial Joulupukki, the bringer of gifts, and his goat-riding elves...

Scandinavian Yule goat figures are often made from straw and decorated with red ribbons.

Goats are known to climb trees!
This nimble goat is perched on an
argan tree in Morocco.

This is a European ash tree. Ash is considered some of the best wood for firewood. It can be split easily with an axe, and burns at a steady rate.

Yule log

The tradition of burning a Yule log comes from the pagan festival of the winter solstice — the longest night of the year — which falls just a few days before Christmas, on 21 or 22 December.

Winter was a cold, dark, and often deadly time for our ancestors in the northern hemisphere. The Vikings and Celts believed that the sun turned the seasons, and when the middle of winter came, it stood still for twelve long days. So a great Yule log would be chosen, huge enough that it would burn throughout those longest nights and shortest days, to conquer the darkness, banish evil spirits, and bring luck for the coming year.

The Yule log would be hauled into the house with great ceremony, and often decorated with mistletoe and evergreens.

Christmas cactus

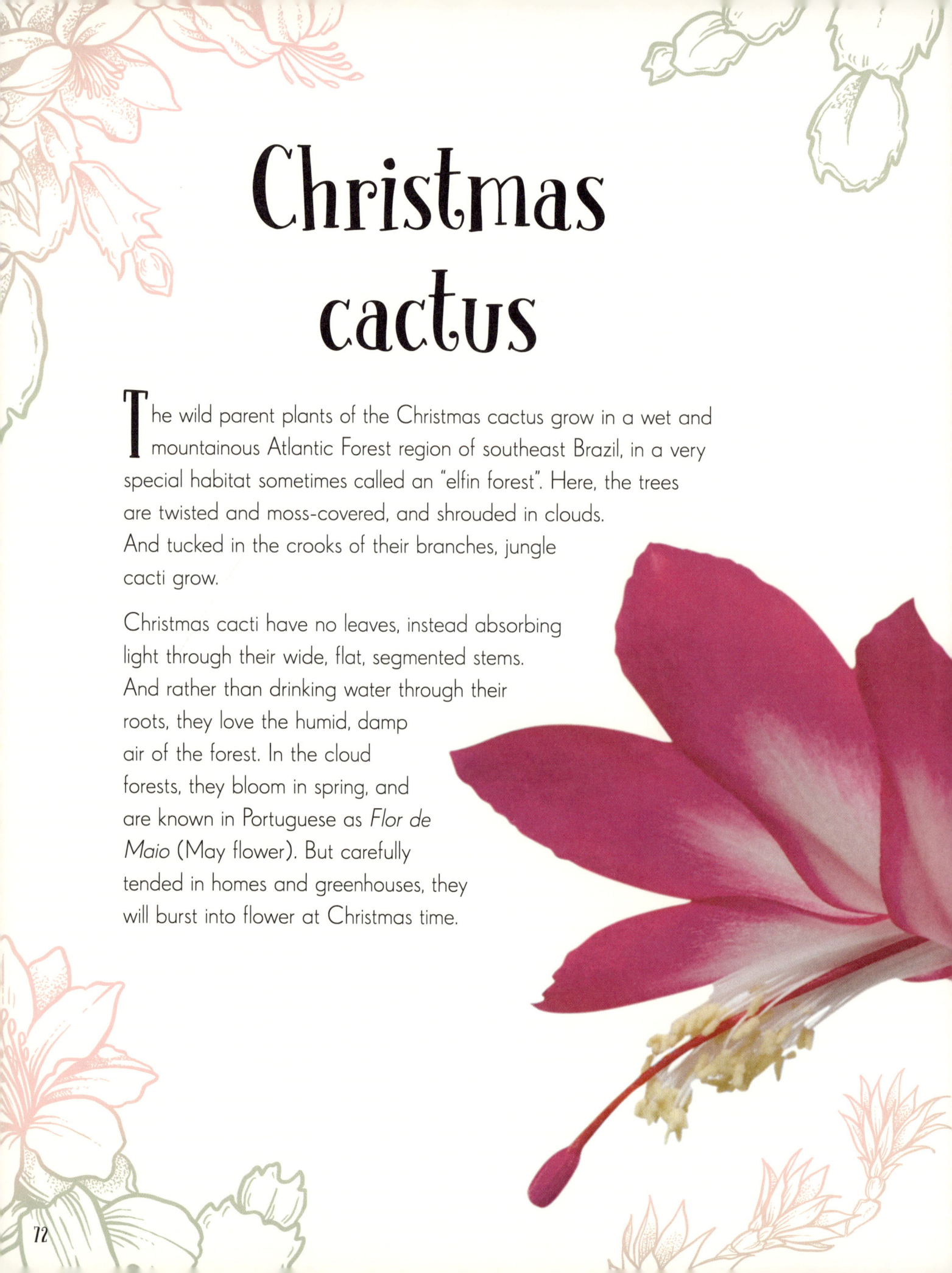

The wild parent plants of the Christmas cactus grow in a wet and mountainous Atlantic Forest region of southeast Brazil, in a very special habitat sometimes called an "elfin forest". Here, the trees are twisted and moss-covered, and shrouded in clouds. And tucked in the crooks of their branches, jungle cacti grow.

Christmas cacti have no leaves, instead absorbing light through their wide, flat, segmented stems. And rather than drinking water through their roots, they love the humid, damp air of the forest. In the cloud forests, they bloom in spring, and are known in Portuguese as *Flor de Maio* (May flower). But carefully tended in homes and greenhouses, they will burst into flower at Christmas time.

Some Christmas cactus plants are passed through families from generation to generation.

The Christmas cactus usually shows off its trumpet-shaped flowers between November and January.

The Spanish and Portuguese Christmas Eve service *Misa de Gallo*, or Mass of the Cockerel, is held when the clock strikes midnight, to celebrate the first cock's crow of Christmas Day.

Cockerel

Before we had clocks, cockerels told us the time. Strutting proudly, with his spurred heels and flamboyant tail feathers, the cockerel crows his loud COCK-A-DOODLE-DOO to protect and guide his flock of hens. He is descended from feathered dinosaurs and jungle fowl, and it is said that if evil spirits walk in the night, the cock's crow will keep them at bay.

The cockerel often crows in the early hours to herald the dawn. Across the world, he is a symbol of light. Amaterasu, the Shinto goddess of the sun, was lured out of hiding by the sound of cocks crowing, restoring light to the world. And, in the mythology of eastern Asia, cockerels announce the coming of great rulers.

Dazzling in colour, the cockerel's scarlet comb regulates his body temperature.

Glossary

alpine From the Alps, high mountain areas in the middle of Europe

ancestors Relatives of people, animals, or plants that lived long ago

antlers Spikes of bone that grow from the skulls of deer, dropping off and growing again each year

archipelago Group of many islands

astrologer Someone who studies the stars, planets, sun, and moon for signs to predict the future

Bedouin Nomadic people who live in desert regions of western Asia and North Africa

Bible Holy book of the Jewish and Christian religions

boreal forest Large area of land covered with trees in the northernmost parts of the world (Canada, Alaska, and Russia)

camouflage Colours or patterns on an animal's skin, fur, or feathers that help it blend in with its natural surroundings

caruncles Loose folds and flaps of skin on a turkey's head and neck, which can grow, shrink, and change colour

cloud forest Type of forest, usually on mountainsides in tropical regions, that has frequent cloud cover

cloven Split into two parts, for example, a sheep or goat's cloven hoof is split into two toes

comb Crown-like ridge of flesh on a chicken's head, usually red, and larger on the male (cockerel)

comet Melting ball of ice and dust travelling through outer space, which leaves a bright trail we can see from earth

conifer Tree or plant that grows cones to protect its seeds

cosmic To do with outer space or the universe, beyond earth's atmosphere

crust Outer layer of the earth

cud Lump of partially digested food that some plant-eating animals (called ruminants) chew for a very long time to get all the goodness out

dormant Special state of rest that some plants and animals can enter to protect themselves from periods of extreme weather

druid Religious leader of the ancient Celtic people

ecosystem Place where animals, plants, soil, and the atmosphere all support one another in a circle of life

egg tooth Sharp little tooth in animals that hatch from eggs; it falls out after they've used it to chip their way through the shell

Epiphany Christian festival to celebrate the Wise Men visiting Jesus, held on either 6 or 19 January

evergreen Plant that keeps its leaves all year round

ferment Process that turns sugars in food into acids or alcohol, and helps it last for longer

Fertile Crescent Lands of western Asia and North Africa around the Nile, Tigris and Euphrates rivers, thought to be where humans first started to farm

foothills Lower slopes or smaller hills around the bottom of a mountain

forage Search for wild food, such as plants, berries, and insects

fractal Pattern that repeats and repeats and never ends

glacier Large mass of ice and snow that moves very slowly, often down a mountain valley

hemisphere Half of the earth: the part north of the equator is the northern hemisphere, and the part south of the equator is the southern hemisphere

hibernation Sleep-like winter state of some animals to help them survive the harsh cold

Indigenous Original peoples from a particular land

Industrial Revolution Period of history from the mid-1700s when the invention of machines changed our ways of living

kernel Soft, edible, inside part of a seed or nut

krill Tiny, shrimp-like sea creatures that are the main source of food for hundreds of ocean animals

Magi Bibilical word for the Wise Men – thought to have been astrologers or kings

mantle Semi-solid layer of the earth between the crust and the core

medieval Historical period from around 1,500 to 725 years ago

Mesoamerica Region that extends from the southern part of North America to Mexico and Central America

meteorite Lump of rock that has come through the earth's atmosphere from outer space

Nativity Biblical word for the event of the birth of Jesus

nectar Sweet liquid made by some flowers to attract birds and insects

Neolithic Time in prehistory when early humans are thought to have first started farming

nomadic People travelling with the seasons from place to place for food and water

Nordic Relating to Norse peoples (Sweden, Denmark, Norway, Finland, Iceland, Faroe Islands, Åland, and Greenland)

Northern Lights Clouds of particles from the sun, visible as coloured streaks of light in the night sky, mainly around the North Pole and sometimes further south

nova Star that suddenly appears very bright in the night sky after interacting with another star and creating a huge explosion

parasite Organism that lives by stealing energy from another living "host" without giving anything in return

parent plant Original plant from which new plants are created

plague Dangerous illness that spreads very easily

pomander Orange with cloves stuck into it, often tied with a red ribbon; also a ball-shaped container for perfumes

pulp Soft, juicy parts of a fruit

Qur'an Holy book of the Islamic religion

resin Thick, sticky liquid made by some trees, especially when they are damaged or cut

segmented Divided into parts

snood Loose flesh that grows out of a turkey's forehead and dangles over its beak

solstice Shortest or longest day of the year: the winter solstice is when our part of the world is furthest from the sun; the summer solstice is when we are closest to the sun

spikelet Small spike that makes up the basic structure of a grass

tailfan Feathers of a bird (such as the male turkey) that can open its tail into a half-circle shape, like a fan

tundra Cold Arctic regions where no trees grow and there is very little rain

vermilion Rich bright-red colour

weevil Beetle with a long pointy snout which it uses to make holes and chew food

Yule winter solstice festival; also used as another word for Christmas

Visual guide

Holly, page 4

Ivy, page 6

Robin redbreast, page 8

Fruits and nuts, page 10

Snow, page 12

Wild boar, page 14

Star of Bethlehem, page 16

Poinsettia, page 18

Reindeer, page 20

Wheat, page 22

Sheep, page 24

Oranges, page 26

Norway spruce, page 28

Christmas trees, page 30

Donkey, page 32

Mistletoe, page 34

Partridge, page 36

Oak, page 38

Amaryllis, page 40

Turkey, page 42

Spices, page 44

Cat, page 46

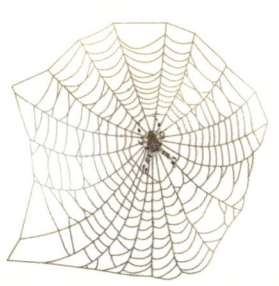

Spider's web, page 48

Cranberries, page 50

Ox, page 52

Northern cardinal, page 54

Coal, page 56

North Pole, page 58

Penguin, page 60

Dove, page 62

Camel, page 64

Three gifts, page 66

Goat, page 68

Yule log, page 70

Christmas cactus, page 72

Cockerel, page 74

Senior editor Marie Greenwood
Senior art editor Roohi Rais
Additional design Nishtha Gupta, Tanya Varkey P
Editorial assistant Anna Bonnerjea
Senior picture researchers Laura Barwick,
Sakshi Saluja
Pre-production designer Pawan Kumar
Pre-production image editor Ashok Kumar
Managing art editors Elle Ward, Ivy Sengupta
Jacket designer Charlotte Jennings
Jacket coordinator Elin Woosnam
Production editor Becky Fallowfield
Senior production controller Inderjit Bhullar
Associate publisher Gemma Farr
Delhi creative head Malavika Talukder

Editorial consultant Phil Hunt

First published in Great Britain in 2025 by
Dorling Kindersley Limited
20 Vauxhall Bridge Road,
London SW1V 2SA

The authorised representative in the EEA is
Dorling Kindersley Verlag GmbH. Arnulfstr. 124,
80636 Munich, Germany

Text copyright © Auriol Bishop 2025
Auriol Bishop has asserted her right to be identified
as the author of this work.
Layout and design copyright © 2025
Dorling Kindersley Limited
A Penguin Random House Company
10 9 8 7 6 5 4 3 2 1
001– 355240–Sept/2025

All rights reserved.
No part of this publication may be reproduced, stored in
or introduced into a retrieval system, or transmitted, in any form,
or by any means (electronic, mechanical, photocopying,
recording, or otherwise), without the prior written permission
of the copyright owner.
No part of this publication may be used or reproduced in
any manner for the purpose of training artificial intelligence
technologies or systems. In accordance with Article 4(3)
of the DSM Directive 2019/790, DK expressly reserves this
work from the text and data mining exception.

A CIP catalogue record for this book
is available from the British Library.
ISBN: 978-0-2417-8201-9
Printed and bound in China

www.dk.com

MIX
Paper | Supporting
responsible forestry
FSC™ C018179

This book was made with Forest
Stewardship Council™ certified
paper – one small step in DK's
commitment to a sustainable future.
For more information go to
www.dk.com/our-green-pledge

DK would like to thank: Olivia Stanford for editorial
support; Vagisha Pushp and Manpreet Kaur for picture
research assistance; Polly Goodman for proofreading; Daniel Long
for the feature illustrations; and Angela Rizza for the pattern and
cover illustrations.

About the author: Auriol Bishop is a storyteller from London whose favourite
stories are about nature. She is the author of *Christmas is Coming: A Treasury
of Simple Ways to Celebrate Festive Days*, as well as the beautifully illustrated
winter storybook *The Bear Who Loved The Moon*, published by Dorling Kindersley.

Picture credits

The publisher would like to thank the following for their kind permission to reproduce their photographs:
(Key: a-above; b-below/bottom; c-centre; f-far; l-left; r-right; t-top)

4-5 Shutterstock.com: Stella Oriente. **6-7 AWL Images:** Mauricio Abreu. **8-9 Dreamstime.com:**
Alantunnicliffe. **10-11 Adobe Stock:** NIKCOA (tc). **Getty Images:** Formatoriginal / 500px (c).
10 Dreamstime.com: Kwanchaichaiudom (cla); Anna Sedneva (bl). **Shutterstock.com:** bigacis (tc).
11 Dreamstime.com: Tamara Kulikova (crb); Viktarm (tr). **Shutterstock.com:** niteenrk (bc). **12-13**
naturepl.com: Sandra Bartocha. **14-15 Alamy Stock Photo:** Duncan Usher. **16-17 Getty Images:**
Felix Ostapenko Photography / 500px. **18 Alamy Stock Photo:** Petr Svarc. **20 AWL Images:** Danita
Delimont Stock (b). **21 AWL Images:** Danita Delimont Stock (b). **22-23 Shutterstock.com:** Artur Kubiak.
24-25 Getty Images / iStock: aksphoto. **26-27 Alamy Stock Photo:** Cro Magnon. **28-29 Alamy Stock Photo:**
imageBROKER / David & Micha Sheldon. **30 Alamy Stock Photo:** piemags / nature (br). **Getty Images / iStock:**
zennie (bl). **31 Alamy Stock Photo:** Paul Pickford (r). **Dreamstime.com:** Nmint (bl). **Getty Images / iStock:**
MediaProduction (tl). **32 Alamy Stock Photo:** Prisma by Dukas Presseagentur GmbH / Schnoz Rene. **34-35**
naturepl.com: Wild Wonders of Europe / Novák. **37 Alamy Stock Photo:** Laurie Campbell. **38-39 Adobe Stock:**
Emvats. **41 Getty Images / iStock:** Griffin24. **42-43 naturepl.com:** George McCarthy. **44 Dreamstime.com:**
Valentyn75 (bl). **Getty Images / iStock:** Olga_Kotsareva (tl). **45 Depositphotos Inc:** Bthnronic (cla). **Dreamstime.
com:** Valentina Razumova (bl); Inna Tarasenko (tr). **Getty Images / iStock:** Gilmanshin (crb). **46-47 Alamy Stock
Photo:** Panther Media GmbH / Astrid08. **48-49 Alamy Stock Photo:** Nature Picture Library / Alex Hyde. **50-51
Getty Images / iStock:** stanley45. **52-53 naturepl.com:** Suzi Eszterhas. **54-55 naturepl.com:** Lynn M. Stone.
56-57 Alamy Stock Photo: Susan E. Degginger. **58-59 Alamy Stock Photo:** Igor Goncharenko. **60 naturepl.com:**
Stefan Christmann. **62-63 Getty Images / iStock:** E+ / proxyminder. **64 Shutterstock.com:** Jan Krava. **66 Alamy
Stock Photo:** Yuen Man Cheung (b). **67 Adobe Stock:** domnitsky (t). **Dreamstime.com:** Colourdream (b).
68-69 Dreamstime.com: Frenta. **70-71 Getty Images:** Moment / Rudolf Vlcek. **72-73 Dreamstime.com:**
Vaeenma. **74-75 naturepl.com:** Klein & Hubert.

Cover images: *Front:* **Adobe Stock:** Duncan Andison cl, by-studio bc; **Alamy Stock Photo:** Zoonar / Karin Jaehne
ca; **Dreamstime.com:** Dewins crb, Irochka tl, Isselee clb, bl, Anna Puhan tr, Valentyn75 cra, Jan Martin Will br,
Svetlana Zhukova tc; **Science Photo Library:** Kenneth Libbrecht cla